P9-CEG-263

_Eg_

No Man's Land

NO MAN'S LAND

by Harold Pinter

GROVE PRESS, INC., NEW YORK

Lad 3-16-11
circ 18

ISBN: 0-394-49931-X
Grove Press ISBN: 0-8021-0101-1

Library of Congress Catalog Card Number: 75-13555

First Printing

Manufactured in the United States of America

Distributed by Random House, Inc., New York

GROVE PRESS, INC., 53 East 11th Street, N.Y., N.Y. 10003

To Jimmy Wax

No Man's Land was first presented by the National Theatre at the Old Vic, Waterloo, London, on 23rd April, 1975, with the following cast:

HIRST, *a man in his sixties*	Ralph Richardson
SPOONER, *a man in his sixties*	John Gielgud
FOSTER, *a man in his thirties*	Michael Feast
BRIGGS, *a man in his forties*	Terence Rigby

Designed by John Bury
Directed by Peter Hall

A large room in a house in North West London.
Well but sparely furnished. A strong and comfortable
straight-backed chair, in which HIRST sits.
A wall of bookshelves, with various items of pottery acting
as bookstands, including two large mugs.

Heavy curtains across the window.

The central feature of the room is an antique cabinet, with
marble top, brass gallery and open shelves, on which stands
a great variety of bottles: spirits, aperitifs, beers, etc.

Act One

Summer.

Night.

SPOONER *stands in the centre of the room.*
He is dressed in a very old and shabby suit, dark faded shirt.
creased spotted tie.

HIRST *is pouring whisky at the cabinet.*
He is precisely dressed. Sports jacket. Well cut trousers.

HIRST

As it is?

SPOONER

As it is, yes please, absolutely as it is.

HIRST *brings him the glass.*

SPOONER

Thank you. How very kind of you. How very kind.

HIRST *pours himself a vodka.*

HIRST

Cheers.

SPOONER

Your health.

They drink. SPOONER *sips.* HIRST *drinks the vodka in one gulp.*
He refills his glass, moves to his chair and sits.
SPOONER *empties his glass.*

HIRST

Please help yourself.

SPOONER

Terribly kind of you.

SPOONER *goes to cabinet, pours. He turns.*

SPOONER

Your good health.

He drinks.

SPOONER

What was it I was saying, as we arrived at your door?

HIRST

Ah . . . let me see.

SPOONER

Yes! I was talking about strength. Do you recall?

HIRST

Strength. Yes.

SPOONER

Yes. I was about to say, you see, that there are some people who appear to be strong, whose idea of what strength consists of is persuasive, but who inhabit the idea and not the fact. What they possess is not strength but expertise. They have nurtured and maintain what is in fact a calculated posture. Half the time it works. It takes a man of intelligence and perception to stick a needle through that posture and discern the essential flabbiness of the stance. I am such a man.

HIRST

You mean one of the latter?

SPOONER

One of the latter, yes, a man of intelligence and perception. Not one of the former, oh no, not at all. By no means.

Pause

May I say how very kind it was of you to ask me in? In fact, you are kindness itself, probably always are kindness itself, now and in England and in Hampstead and for all eternity.

He looks about the room.

What a remarkably pleasant room. I feel at peace here. Safe from all danger. But please don't be alarmed. I shan't stay long. I never stay long, with others. They do not wish it. And that, for me, is a happy state of affairs. My only security, you see, my true comfort and solace, rests in the confirmation that I elicit from people of all kinds a common and constant level of indifference. It assures me that I am as I think myself to be, that I am fixed, concrete. To show interest in me or, good gracious, anything tending towards a positive liking of me, would cause in me a condition of the acutest alarm. Fortunately, the danger is remote.

Pause

I speak to you with this startling candour because you are clearly a reticent man, which appeals, and because you are a stranger to me, and because you are clearly kindness itself.

Pause

Do you often hang about Hampstead Heath?

HIRST

No.

SPOONER

But on your excursions . . however rare . . on your rare excursions . . you hardly expect to run into the likes of me? I take it?

HIRST

Hardly.

SPOONER

I often hang about Hampstead Heath myself, expecting nothing. I'm too old for any kind of expectation. Don't you agree?

HIRST

Yes.

SPOONER

A pitfall and snare, if ever there was one. But of course I observe a good deal, on my peeps through twigs. A wit once entitled me a betwixt twig peeper. A most clumsy construction, I thought.

HIRST

Infelicitous.

SPOONER

My Christ you're right.

Pause

HIRST

What a wit.

SPOONER

You're most acutely right. All we have left is the English language. Can it be salvaged? That is my question.

HIRST

You mean in what rests its salvation?

SPOONER

More or less.

HIRST

Its salvation must rest in you.

SPOONER

It's uncommonly kind of you to say so. In you too, perhaps, although I haven't sufficient evidence to go on, as yet.

Pause

HIRST

You mean because I've said little?

SPOONER

You're a quiet one. It's a great relief. Can you imagine two of us gabbling away like me? It would be intolerable.

Pause

By the way, with reference to peeping, I do feel it incumbent upon me to make one thing clear. I don't peep on sex. That's gone forever. You follow me? When my twigs happen to shall I say rest their peep on sexual conjugations, however periphrastic, I see only whites of eyes, so close, they glut me, no distance possible, and when you can't keep the proper distance between yourself and others, when you can no longer maintain an objective relation to matter, the game's not worth the candle, so forget it and remember that what is obligatory to keep in your vision is space, space in moonlight particularly, and lots of it.

HIRST

You speak with the weight of experience behind you.

SPOONER

And beneath me. Experience is a paltry thing. Everyone has it and will tell his tale of it. I leave experience to psychological interpreters, the wetdream world. I myself can do any graph of experience you wish, to suit your taste or mine. Child's play. The present is truly unscrupulous. I am a poet. I am interested in where I am eternally present and active.

HIRST *stands, goes to cabinet, pours vodka.*

I have gone too far, you think?

HIRST

I'm expecting you to go very much further.

SPOONER

Really? That doesn't mean I interest you, I hope?

HIRST

Not in the least.

SPOONER

Thank goodness for that. For a moment my heart sank.

HIRST *draws the curtains aside, looks out briefly, lets curtain fall, remains standing.*

But nevertheless you're right. Your instinct is sound. I could go further, in more ways than one. I could advance, reserve my defences, throw on a substitute, call up the cavalry, embody in essence Von Kleist's retreat from the Caucasus (the wittiest and

most subtle systematic withdrawal known to man) or throw
everything forward out of the knowledge that when joy over-
floweth there can be no holding of joy. The point I'm trying
to make, in case you've missed it, is that I am a free man.

HIRST *pours himself another vodka and drinks it. He puts the*
glass down, moves carefully to his chair, sits.

                            HIRST
It's a long time since we had a free man in this house.

                            SPOONER
We?

                            HIRST
I.

                            SPOONER
Is there another?

                            HIRST
Another what?

                            SPOONER
People. Person.

                            HIRST
What other?

                            SPOONER
There are two mugs on that shelf.

                            HIRST
The second is for you.

SPOONER

And the first?

HIRST

Would you like to use it? Would you like some hot refreshment?

SPOONER

That would be dangerous. I'll stick to your scotch, if I may.

HIRST

Help yourself.

SPOONER

Thank you.

He goes to cabinet.

HIRST

I'll take a whisky with you, if you would be so kind.

SPOONER

With pleasure. Weren't you drinking vodka?

HIRST

I'll be happy to join you in a whisky.

SPOONER *pours.*

SPOONER

You'll take it as it is, as it comes?

HIRST

Oh, absolutely as it comes.

SPOONER *brings* HIRST *his glass.*

                    SPOONER
Your very good health.

                    HIRST
Yours.

They drink.

Tell me . . . do you often hang about Jack Straw's Castle?

                    SPOONER
I knew it as a boy.

                    HIRST
Do you find it as beguiling a public house now as it was in the
days of the highwaymen, when it was frequented by highwaymen? Notably Jack Straw. The great Jack Straw. Do you find
it much changed?

                    SPOONER
It changed my life.

                    HIRST
Good Lord. Did it really?

                    SPOONER
I refer to a midsummer night, when I shared a drink with a
Hungarian émigré, lately retired from Paris.

                    HIRST
The same drink?

SPOONER

By no means. You've guessed, I would imagine, that he was an
erstwhile member of the Hungarian aristocracy?

HIRST

I did guess, yes.

SPOONER

On that summer evening, led by him, I first appreciated how
quiet life can be, in the midst of yahoos and hullabaloos. He
exerted on me a quite uniquely . . . calming influence, without
exertion, without any . . . desire to influence. He was so much
older than me. My expectations in those days, and I confess I
had expectations in those days, did not include him in their
frame of reference. I'd meandered over to Hampstead Heath,
a captive to memories of a more than usually pronounced
grisliness, and found myself, not much to my surprise, order-
ing a pint at the bar of Jack Straw's Castle. This achieved, and
having negotiated a path through a particularly repellent lick-
spittling herd of literati, I stumbled, unseeing, with my pint,
to his bald, tanned, unmoving table. How bald he was.

Pause

I think, after quite half my pint had descended, never to be
savoured again, that I spoke, suddenly, suddenly spoke, and
received . . . a response, no other word will do, a response, the
like of which –

HIRST

What was he drinking?

SPOONER

What?

HIRST

What was he drinking?

SPOONER

Pernod.

Pause

I was impressed, more or less at that point, by an intuition that he possessed a measure of serenity the like of which I had never encountered.

HIRST

What did he say?

SPOONER *stares at him.*

SPOONER

You expect me to remember what he said?

HIRST

No.

Pause

SPOONER

What he said . . . all those years ago . . . is neither here nor there. It was not what he said but possibly the way he sat which has remained with me all my life and has, I am quite sure, made me what I am.

Pause

And I met you at the same pub tonight, although at a different table.

Pause

And I wonder at you, now, as once I wondered at him. But will I wonder at you tomorrow, I wonder, as I still wonder at him today?

HIRST

I cannot say.

SPOONER

It cannot be said.

Pause

I'll ask you another question. Have you any idea from what I derive my strength?

HIRST

Strength? No.

SPOONER

I have never been loved. From this I derive my strength. Have you? Ever? Been loved?

HIRST

Oh, I don't suppose so.

SPOONER

I looked up once into my mother's face. What I saw there was nothing less than pure malevolence. I was fortunate to escape with my life. You will want to know what I had done to provoke such hatred in my own mother.

HIRST

You'd pissed yourself.

SPOONER

Quite right. How old do you think I was at the time?

HIRST

Twenty eight.

SPOONER

Quite right. However, I left home soon after.

Pause

My mother remains, I have to say, a terribly attractive woman
in many ways. Her buns are the best.

HIRST *looks at him.*

Her currant buns. The best.

HIRST

Would you be so kind as to pour me another drop of whisky?

SPOONER

Certainly.

SPOONER *takes the glass, pours whisky into it, gives it to* HIRST.

SPOONER

Perhaps it's about time I introduced myself. My name is
Spooner.

HIRST

Ah.

SPOONER

I'm a staunch friend of the arts, particularly the art of poetry,
and a guide to the young. I keep open house. Young poets

come to me. They read me their verses. I comment, give them
coffee, make no charge. Women are admitted, some of whom
are also poets. Some are not. Some of the men are not. Most of
the men are not. But with the windows open to the garden,
my wife pouring long glasses of squash, with ice, on a summer
evening, young voices occasionally lifted in unaccompanied
ballad, young bodies lying in the dying light, my wife moving
through the shadows in her long gown, what can ail? I mean
who can gainsay us? What quarrel can be found with what is,
au fond, a gesture towards the sustenance and preservation of
art, and through art to virtue?

HIRST
Through art to virtue. (*Raises glass.*) To your continued health.

SPOONER *sits, for the first time.*

SPOONER
When we had our cottage . . . when we had our cottage . . . we
gave our visitors tea, on the lawn.

HIRST
I did the same.

SPOONER
On the lawn?

HIRST
I did the same.

SPOONER
You had a cottage?

HIRST

Tea on the lawn.

SPOONER

What happened to them? What happened to our cottages?
What happened to our lawns?

Pause

Be frank. Tell me. You've revealed something. You've made an
unequivocal reference to your past. Don't go back on it. We
share something. A memory of the bucolic life. We're both
English.

Pause

HIRST

In the village church, the beams are hung with garlands, in
honour of young women of the parish, reputed to have died
virgin.

Pause

However, the garlands are not bestowed on maidens only, but
on all who die unmarried, wearing the white flower of a blame-
less life.

Pause

SPOONER

You mean that not only young women of the parish but also
young men of the parish are so honoured?

HIRST

I do.

SPOONER

And that old men of the parish who also died maiden are so garlanded?

HIRST

Certainly.

SPOONER

I am enraptured. Tell me more. Tell me more about the quaint little perversions of your life and times. Tell me more, with all the authority and brilliance you can muster, about the socio-economic-political structure of the environment in which you attained to the age of reason. Tell me more.

Pause

HIRST

There is no more.

SPOONER

Tell me then about your wife.

HIRST

What wife?

SPOONER

How beautiful she was, how tender and how true. Tell me with what speed she swung in the air, with what velocity she came off the wicket, whether she was responsive to finger spin, whether you could bowl a shooter with her, or an offbreak with a legbreak action. In other words, did she google?

Silence

You will not say. I will tell you then . . . that my wife . . . had everything. Eyes, a mouth, hair, teeth, buttocks, breasts, absolutely everything. And legs.

HIRST

Which carried her away.

SPOONER

Carried who away? Yours or mine?

Pause

Is she here now, your wife? Cowering in a locked room, perhaps?

Pause

Was she ever here? Was she ever there, in your cottage? It is my duty to tell you you have failed to convince. I am an honest and intelligent man. You pay me less than my due. Are you, equally, being fair to the lady? I begin to wonder whether truly accurate and therefore essentially poetic definition means anything to you at all. I begin to wonder whether you do in fact truly remember her, whether you truly did love her, truly caressed her, truly did cradle her, truly did husband her, falsely dreamed or did truly adore her. I have seriously questioned these propositions and find them threadbare.

Silence

Her eyes, I take it, were hazel?

HIRST *stands, carefully. He moves, with a slight stagger, to the cabinet, pours whisky, drinks.*

HIRST

Hazel shit.

SPOONER

Good lord, good lord, do I detect a touch of the maudlin?

Pause

Hazel shit. I ask myself: Have I ever seen hazel shit? Or hazel eyes, for that matter?

HIRST *throws his glass at him, ineffectually. It bounces on the carpet.*

Do I detect a touch of the hostile? Do I detect – with respect – a touch of too many glasses of ale followed by the great malt which wounds? Which wounds?

Silence

HIRST

Tonight . . . my friend . . . you find me in the last lap of a race . . . I had long forgotten to run.

Pause

SPOONER

A metaphor. Things are looking up.

Pause

I would say, albeit on a brief acquaintance, that you lack the essential quality of manliness, which is to put your money

where your mouth is, to pick up a pintpot and know it to be a
pintpot, and knowing it to be a pintpot, to declare it as a pintpot, and to stay faithful to that pintpot as though you had given
birth to it out of your own arse. You lack that capability, in my
view.

Pause

Do forgive me my candour. It is not method but madness. So
you won't, I hope, object if I take out my prayer beads and
my prayer mat and salute what I take to be your impotence?

He stands.

I salute. And attend. And saluting and attending am at your
service all embracing. Heed me. I am a relevant witness. And
could be a friend.

HIRST *grips the cabinet, rigid.*

You need a friend. You have a long hike, my lad, up which,
presently, you slog unfriended. Let me perhaps be your boat-
man. For if and when we talk of a river we talk of a deep and
dank architecture. In other words, never disdain a helping
hand, especially one of such rare quality. And it is not only the
quality of my offer which is rare, it is the act itself, the offer
itself – quite without precedent. I offer myself to you as a
friend. Think before you speak. For this proposition, after
thought, will I assure you be seen to be carte blanche, open
sesame and worthy the tender, for it is an expression of a quite
unique generosity and I make it knowingly.

HIRST *attempts to move, stops, grips the cabinet.*

Remember this. You've lost your wife of hazel hue, you've lost her and what can you do, she will no more come back to you, with a tillifola tillifola tillifoladi-foladi-foloo.

HIRST
No.

Pause

No man's land . . . does not move . . . or change . . . or grow old . . . remains . . . forever . . . icy . . . silent.

HIRST *loosens his grip on the cabinet, staggers, across the room, holds on to a chair.*

He waits, moves, falls.

He waits, gets to his feet, moves, falls.

SPOONER *watches.*

HIRST *crawls towards the door, manages to open it, crawls out of the door.*

SPOONER *remains still.*

SPOONER
I have known this before. The exit through the door, by way of belly and floor.

He looks at the room, walks about it, looking at each object closely, stops, hands behind his back, surveying the room.

A door, somewhere in the house, closes.

Silence.

The front door opens, and slams sharply.

SPOONER *stiffens, is still.*

FOSTER *enters the room. He is casually dressed.*

He stops still upon seeing SPOONER. *He stands, looking at* SPOONER.

Silence

FOSTER

What are you drinking? Christ I'm thirsty. How are you? I'm parched.

He goes to cabinet, opens a bottle of beer, pours.

What are you drinking? It's bloody late. I'm worn to a frazzle. This is what I want. (*He drinks.*) Taxi? No chance. Taxi drivers are against me. Something about me. Some unknown factor. My gait, perhaps. Or perhaps because I travel incognito. Oh, that's better. Works wonders. How are you? What are you drinking? Who are you? I thought I'd never make it. What a hike. And not only that. I'm defenceless. I don't carry a gun in London. But I'm not bothered. Once you've done the East you've done it all. I've done the East. But I still like a nice lighthouse like this one. Have you met your host? He's my father. It was our night off tonight, you see. He was going to stay at home, listen to some lieder. I hope he had a quiet and pleasant evening. Who are you, by the way? What are you drinking?

SPOONER

I'm a friend of his.

FOSTER

You're not typical.

BRIGGS *comes into the room, stops. He is casually dressed, stocky.*

BRIGGS

Who's this?

FOSTER

His name's Friend. This is Mr. Briggs. Mr. Friend – Mr. Briggs. I'm Mr. Foster. Old English stock. John Foster. Jack. Jack Foster. Old English name. Foster. John Foster. Jack Foster. Foster. This man's name is Briggs.

Pause

BRIGGS

I've seen Mr. Friend before.

FOSTER

Seen him before?

BRIGGS

I know him.

FOSTER

Do you really?

BRIGGS

I've seen you before.

SPOONER

Possibly, possibly.

BRIGGS

Yes. You collect the beermugs from the tables in a pub in Chalk Farm.

SPOONER

The landlord's a friend of mine. When he's shorthanded, I give him a helping hand.

BRIGGS

Who says the landlord's a friend of yours?

FOSTER

He does.

BRIGGS

I'm talking about The Bull's Head in Chalk Farm.

SPOONER

Yes, yes. So am I.

BRIGGS

So am I.

FOSTER

I know The Bull's Head. The landlord's a friend of mine.

BRIGGS

He collects the mugs.

FOSTER

A firstclass pub. I've known the landlord for years.

BRIGGS

He says he's a friend of the landlord.

FOSTER

He says he's a friend of our friend too.

BRIGGS

What friend?

FOSTER

Our host.

BRIGGS

He's a bloody friend of everyone then.

FOSTER

He's everybody's bloody friend. How many friends have you got altogether, Mr. Friend?

BRIGGS

He probably couldn't count them.

FOSTER

Well, there's me too, now. I'm another one of your new friends. I'm your newest new friend. Not him. Not Briggs. He's nobody's fucking friend. People tend to be a little wary of Briggs. They balk at giving him their all. But me they like at first sight.

BRIGGS

Sometimes they love you at first sight.

FOSTER

Sometimes they do. That's why, when I travel, I get all the gold, nobody offers me dross. People take an immediate shine to me, especially women, especially in Siam or Bali. He knows I'm not a liar. Tell him about the Siamese girls.

BRIGGS

They loved him at first sight.

FOSTER

(*To* SPOONER.) You're not Siamese though, are you?

BRIGGS

He's a very long way from being Siamese.

FOSTER

Ever been out there?

SPOONER

I've been to Amsterdam.

FOSTER *and* BRIGGS *stare at him.*

I mean that was the last place . . . I visited. I know Europe well.
My name is Spooner, by the way. Yes, one afternoon in
Amsterdam . . . I was sitting outside a café by a canal. The
weather was superb. At another table, in shadow, was a man
whistling under his breath, sitting very still, almost rigid. At
the side of the canal was a fisherman. He caught a fish. He
lifted it high. The waiter cheered and applauded, the two men,
the waiter and the fisherman, laughed. A little girl, passing,
laughed. Two lovers, passing, kissed. The fish was lofted, on the
rod. The fish and the rod glinted in the sun, as they swayed.
The fisherman's cheeks were flushed, with pleasure. I decided
to paint a picture – of the canal, the waiter, the child, the
fisherman, the lovers, the fish, and in background, in shadow,
the man at the other table, and to call it The Whistler. The
Whistler. If you had seen the picture, and the title, would the
title have baffled you?

Pause

FOSTER

(*To* BRIGGS.) Do you want to answer that question?

BRIGGS

No. Go on. You answer it.

FOSTER

Well, speaking for myself, I think I would have been baffled by that title. But I might have appreciated the picture. I might even have been grateful for it.

Pause

Did you hear what I said? I might have been grateful for the picture. A good work of art tends to move me. You follow me? I'm not a cunt, you know.

Pause

I'm very interested to hear you're a painter. You do it in your spare time, I suppose?

SPOONER

Quite.

FOSTER

Did you ever paint that picture, The Whistler?

SPOONER

Not yet, I'm afraid.

FOSTER

Don't leave it too long. You might lose the inspiration.

BRIGGS

Ever painted a beermug?

SPOONER

You must come and see my collection, any time you wish.

BRIGGS

What of, beermugs?

SPOONER

No, no. Paintings.

FOSTER

Where do you keep it?

SPOONER

At my house in the country. You would receive the warmest of welcomes.

FOSTER

Who from?

SPOONER

My wife. My two daughters.

FOSTER

Really? Would they like me? What do you think? Would they love me at first sight?

SPOONER

(*Laughing*.) Quite possibly.

FOSTER

What about him?

SPOONER *looks at* BRIGGS.

SPOONER

They are remarkably gracious women.

FOSTER

You're a lucky man. What are you drinking?

SPOONER

Scotch.

FOSTER *goes to cabinet, pours scotch, stands holding glass.*

FOSTER

What do you make of this? When I was out East . . . once . . a
kind of old stinking tramp, bollock naked, asked me for a few
bob. I didn't know him. He was a complete stranger. But I
could see immediately he wasn't a man to trust. He had a dog
with him. They only had about one eye between them. So I
threw him some sort of coin. He caught this bloody coin,
looked at it with a bit of disaste, and then he threw the coin
back. Well, automatically I went to catch it, I clutched at it,
but the bloody coin disappeared into thin air. It didn't drop
anywhere. It just disappeared . . into thin air . . on its way
towards me. He then let out a few curses and pissed off, with
his dog. Oh, here's your whisky, by the way. (*Hands it to him.*)
What do you make of that incident?

SPOONER

He was a con artist.

FOSTER

Do you think so?

SPOONER

You would be wise to grant the event no integrity whatsoever.

FOSTER

You don't subscribe to the mystery of the Orient?

SPOONER

A typical Eastern contrick.

FOSTER

Double Dutch, you mean?

SPOONER

Certainly. Your good health. (*Drinks.*)

HIRST *enters, wearing a dressing-gown.*

BRIGGS *goes to cabinet, pours whisky.*

HIRST

I can't sleep. I slept briefly. I think. Perhaps it was sufficient.
Yes. I woke up, out of a dream. I feel cheerful. Who'll give me
a glass of whisky?

HIRST *sits.* BRIGGS *brings him whisky.*

My goodness, is this for me? How did you know? You knew.
You're very sensitive. Cheers. The first today. What day is it?
What's the time? Is it still night?

BRIGGS

Yes.

HIRST

The same night? I was dreaming of a waterfall. No, no, of a
lake. I think it was . . just recently. Can you remember when I
went to bed? Was it daylight? It's good to go to sleep in the

late afternoon. After tea and toast. You hear the faint begin-
nings of the evening sounds, and then nothing. Everywhere
else people are changing for dinner. You're tucked up, the
shutters closed, gaining a march on the world.

He passes his glass to BRIGGS, *who fills and returns it.*

Something is depressing me. What is it? It was the dream, yes.
Waterfalls. No, no, a lake. Water. Drowning. Not me. Someone else. How nice to have company. Can you imagine waking
up, finding no-one here, just furniture, staring at you? Most
unpleasant. I've known that condition, I've been through that
period – cheers – I came round to human beings in the end.
Like yourselves. A wise move. I tried laughing alone. Pathetic.
Have you all got drinks?

He looks at SPOONER.

Who's that? A friend of yours? Won't someone introduce me?

FOSTER
He's a friend of yours.

HIRST
In the past I knew remarkable people. I've a photograph album
somewhere. I'll find it. You'll be impressed by the faces. Very
handsome. Sitting on grass with hampers. I had a moustache.
Quite a few of my friends had moustaches. Remarkable faces.
Remarkable moustaches. What was it informed the scene?
A tenderness towards our fellows, perhaps. The sun shone. The
girls had lovely hair, dark, sometimes red. Under their dresses
their bodies were white. It's all in my album. I'll find it. You'll
be struck by the charm of the girls, their grace, the ease with
which they sit, pour tea, loll. It's all in my album.

He empties glass, holds it up.

Who is the kindest among you?

BRIGGS *takes glass to cabinet.*

Thank you. What would I do without the two of you? I'd sit
here forever, waiting for a stranger to fill up my glass. What
would I do while I waited? Look through my album? Make
plans for the future?

BRIGGS

(*Bringing glass.*) You'd crawl to the bottle and stuff it between
your teeth.

HIRST

No. I drink with dignity.

He drinks, looks at SPOONER.

Who is this man? Do I know him?

FOSTER

He says he's a friend of yours.

HIRST

My true friends look out at me from my album. I had my
world. I have it. Don't think now that it's gone I'll choose to
sneer at it, to cast doubt on it, to wonder if it properly existed.
No. We're talking of my youth, which can never leave me. No.
It existed. It was solid, the people in it were solid, while . . .
transformed by light, while being sensitive . . . to all the changing light.

When I stood my shadow fell upon her. She looked up.
Give me the bottle. Give me the bottle.

BRIGGS *gives him the bottle. He drinks from it.*

It's gone. Did it exist? It's gone. It never existed. It remains.

I am sitting here forever.

How kind of you. I wish you'd tell me what the weather's
like. I wish you'd damnwell tell me what night it is, this night
or the next night or the other one, the night before last. Be
frank. Is it the night before last?

Help yourselves. I hate drinking alone. There's too much
solitary shittery.

What was it? Shadows. Brightness, through leaves. Gam-
bolling. In the bushes. Young lovers. A fall of water. It was my
dream. The lake. Who was drowning in my dream?

It was blinding. I remember it. I've forgotten. By all that's
sacred and holy. The sounds stopped. It was freezing. There's a
gap in me. I can't fill it. There's a flood running through me.
I can't plug it. They're blotting me out. Who is doing it? I'm
suffocating. It's a muff. A muff, perfumed. Someone is doing
me to death.

She looked up. I was staggered. I had never seen anything so
beautiful. That's all poison. We can't be expected to live like
that.

I remember nothing. I'm sitting in this room. I see you all,
every one of you. A sociable gathering. The dispositions are
kindly.

Am I asleep? There's no water. No-one is drowning.

Yes; yes, come on, come on, come on, pipe up, speak up, speak up, speak up, you're fucking me about, you bastards, ghosts, long ghosts, you're making noises, I can hear you humming, I wear a crisp blue shirt at the Ritz, I wear a crisp blue shirt at the Ritz, I know him well, the wine waiter, Boris, Boris, he's been there for years, blinding shadows, then a fall of water –

SPOONER

It was I drowning in your dream.

HIRST *falls to the floor. They all go to him.*
FOSTER *turns to* SPOONER.

FOSTER

Bugger off.

BRIGGS *pulls* HIRST *up.* HIRST *wards him off.*

HIRST

Unhand me.

He stands erect. SPOONER *moves to him.*

SPOONER

He has grandchildren. As have I. As I have. We both have fathered. We are of an age. I know his wants. Let me take his arm. Respect our age. Come, I'll seat you.

He takes HIRST's *arm and leads him to a chair.*

There's no pity in these people.

FOSTER

Christ.

SPOONER

I am your true friend. That is why your dream . . . was so
distressing. You saw me drowning in your dream. But have no
fear. I am not drowned.

FOSTER

Christ.

SPOONER

(*To* HIRST.) Would you like me to make you some coffee?

BRIGGS

He thinks he's a waiter in Amsterdam.

FOSTER

Service non compris.

BRIGGS

Whereas he's a pintpot attendant in The Bull's Head. And a
pisspot attendant as well.

FOSTER

Our host must have been in The Bull's Head tonight, where
he had an unfortunate encounter. (*To* SPOONER.) Hey scout, I
think there's been some kind of misunderstanding. You're not
in some shithouse down by the docks. You're in the home of a
man of means, of a man of achievement. Do you understand
me?

He turns to BRIGGS.

Why am I bothering? Tell me. Eh?

He turns back to SPOONER.

Listen chummybum. We protect this gentleman against corruption, against men of craft, against men of evil, we could
destroy you without a glance, we take care of this gentleman,
we do it out of love.

He turns to BRIGGS.

Why am I talking to him? I'm wasting my time with a non-
starter. I must be going mad. I don't usually talk. I don't have
to. Normally I keep quiet.

He turns back to SPOONER.

I know what it is. There's something about you fascinates me.

SPOONER

It's my bearing.

FOSTER

That's what it must be.

BRIGGS

I've seen Irishmen chop his balls off.

FOSTER

I suppose once you've had Irishmen you've had everything.
(*To* SPOONER.) Listen. Keep it tidy. You follow? You've just
laid your hands on a rich and powerful man. It's not what
you're used to, scout. How can I make it clear? This is another
class. It's another realm of operation. It's a world of silk.
It's a world of organdie. It's a world of flower arrangements.
It's a world of eighteenth century cookery books. It's nothing
to do with toffeeapples and a packet of crisps. It's milk in the
bath. It's the cloth bellpull. It's organisation.

BRIGGS

It's not rubbish.

FOSTER

It's not rubbish. We deal in originals. Nothing duff, nothing ersatz, we don't open any old bottle of brandy. Mind you don't fall into a quicksand. (*To* BRIGGS.) Why don't I kick his head off and have done with it?

SPOONER

I'm the same age as your master. I used to picnic in the country too, at the same time as he.

FOSTER

Listen, my friend. This man in this chair, he's a creative man. He's an artist. We make life possible for him. We're in a position of trust. Don't try to drive a wedge into a happy household. You understand me? Don't try to make a nonsense out of family life.

BRIGGS

(*To* FOSTER.) If you can't, I can.

He moves to SPOONER *and beckons to him, with his forefinger.*

BRIGGS

Come here.

HIRST

Where are the sandwiches? Cut the bread.

BRIGGS

It's cut.

HIRST

It is not cut. Cut it!

BRIGGS *stands still.*

BRIGGS

I'll go and cut it.

He leaves the room.

HIRST

(*To* SPOONER.) I know you from somewhere.

FOSTER

I must clean the house. No-one else'll do it. Your financial adviser is coming to breakfast. I've got to think about that. His taste changes from day to day. One day he wants boiled eggs and toast, the next day orange juice and poached eggs, the next scrambled eggs and smoked salmon, the next a mushroom omelette and champagne. Any minute now it'll be dawn. A new day. Your financial adviser's dreaming of his breakfast. He's dreaming of eggs. Eggs, eggs. What kind of eggs? I'm exhausted. I've been up all night. But it never stops. Nothing stops. It's all fizz. This is my life. I have my brief arousals. They leave me panting. I can't take the pace in London. Nobody knows what I miss.

BRIGGS *enters and stands, listening.*

I miss the Siamese girls. I miss the girls in Bali. You don't come across them over here. You see them occasionally, on the steps of language schools, they're learning English, they're not prepared to have a giggle and a cuddle in their own language. Not in Regent street. A giggle and a cuddle. Sometimes

my ambitions extend no further than that. I could do something else. I could make another life. I don't have to waste my
time looking after a pisshound. I could find the right niche and
be happy. The right niche, the right happiness.

BRIGGS

We're out of bread. I'm looking at the housekeeper. Neurotic
poof. He prefers idleness. Unspeakable ponce. He prefers the
Malay Straits, where they give you hot toddy in a fourposter.
He's nothing but a vagabond cock. (*To* SPOONER.) Move over.

SPOONER *moves out of his way.*

BRIGGS

(*To* HIRST.) Get up.

HIRST *slowly stands.* BRIGGS *leads him to the door.*

BRIGGS

(*To* HIRST.) Keep on the move. Don't look back.

HIRST

I know that man.

BRIGGS *leads* HIRST *out of the room.*

Silence

FOSTER

Do you know what I saw once in the desert, in the Australian
desert? A man walking along carrying two umbrellas. Two
umbrellas. In the outback.

Pause

                    SPOONER

Was it raining?

                    FOSTER

No. It was a beautiful day. I nearly asked him what he was up
to but I changed my mind.

                    SPOONER

Why?

                    FOSTER

Well, I decided he must be some kind of lunatic. I thought he
would only confuse me.

FOSTER *walks about the room, stops at the door.*

Listen. You know what it's like when you're in a room with the
light on and then suddenly the light goes out? I'll show you.
It's like this.

He turns the light out.

BLACKOUT

Act Two

Morning

SPOONER *is alone in the room. The curtains are still closed, but shafts of light enter the room.*

He is sitting.

He stands, goes slowly to door, tries handle, with fatigue, withdraws.

SPOONER
I have known this before. Morning. A locked door. A house of silence and strangers.

He sits, shivers.

The door is unlocked. BRIGGS *comes in, key in hand. He is wearing a suit. He opens the curtains. Daylight.*

BRIGGS
I've been asked to inquire if you're hungry.

SPOONER
Food? I never touch it.

BRIGGS
The financial adviser didn't turn up. You can have his breakfast. He phoned his order through, then phoned again to cancel the appointment.

SPOONER
For what reason?

BRIGGS

Jack spoke to him, not me.

SPOONER

What reason did he give your friend?

BRIGGS

Jack said he said he found himself without warning in the centre of a vast aboriginal financial calamity.

Pause

SPOONER

He clearly needs an adviser.

Pause

BRIGGS

I won't bring you breakfast if you're going to waste it.

SPOONER

I abhor waste.

BRIGGS *goes out.*

I have known this before. The door unlocked. The entrance of a stranger. The offer of alms. The shark in the harbour.

Silence

BRIGGS *enters carrying a tray. On the tray are breakfast dishes covered by silver lids and a bottle of champagne in a bucket.*

He places the tray on a small table and brings a chair to the table.

BRIGGS

Scrambled eggs. Shall I open the champagne?

SPOONER

Is it cold?

BRIGGS

Freezing.

SPOONER

Please open it.

BRIGGS *begins to open bottle.* SPOONER *lifts lids, peers, sets lids aside, butters toast.*

SPOONER

Who is the cook?

BRIGGS

We share all burdens, Jack and myself.

BRIGGS *pours champagne. Offers glass.* SPOONER *sips.*

Pause

SPOONER

Thank you.

SPOONER *begins to eat.* BRIGGS *draws up a chair to the table and sits, watching.*

BRIGGS

We're old friends, Jack and myself. We met at a street corner.
I should tell you he'll deny this account. His story will be
different. I was standing at a street corner. A car drew up. It
was him. He asked me the way to Bolsover street. I told him
Bolsover street was in the middle of an intricate one-way system. It was a one-way system easy enough to get into. The
only trouble was that, once in, you couldn't get out. I told him
his best bet, if he really wanted to get to Bolsover street, was to
take the first left, first right, second right, third on the left,
keep his eye open for a hardware shop, go right round the
square, keeping to the inside lane, take the second Mews on the
right and then stop. He will find himself facing a very tall
office block, with a crescent courtyard. He can take advantage
of this office block. He can go round the crescent, come out the
other way, follow the arrows, go past two sets of traffic lights
and take the next left indicated by the first green filter he
comes across. He's got the Post Office Tower in his vision the
whole time. All he's got to do is to reverse into the under-
ground car park, change gear, go straight on, and he'll find
himself in Bolsover street with no trouble at all. I did warn
him, though, that he'll still be faced with the problem, having
found Bolsover street, of losing it. I told him I knew one or two
people who'd been wandering up and down Bolsover street for
years. They'd wasted their bloody youth there. The people
who live there, their faces are grey, they're in a state of despair,
but nobody pays any attention, you see. All people are worried
about is their illgotten gains. I wrote to The Times about it.
Life At A Dead End, I called it. Went for nothing. Anyway,
I told him that probably the best thing he could do was to
forget the whole idea of getting to Bolsover street. I remember
saying to him: This trip you've got in mind, drop it, it could
prove fatal. But he said he had to deliver a parcel. Anyway, I
took all this trouble with him because he had a nice open face.

He looked like a man who would always do good to others himself. Normally I wouldn't give a fuck. I should tell you he'll deny this account. His story will be different.

SPOONER *places the lid on his plate.*

BRIGGS *pours champagne into* SPOONER's *glass.*

When did you last have champagne for breakfast?

SPOONER
Well, to be quite honest, I'm a champagne drinker.

BRIGGS
Oh, are you?

SPOONER
I know my wines. (*He drinks.*) Dijon. In the thirties. I made many trips to Dijon, for the winetasting, with my French translator. Even after his death, I continued to go to Dijon, until I could go no longer.

Pause

Hugo. A good companion.

Pause.

You will wonder of course what he translated. The answer is my verse. I am a poet.

Pause

BRIGGS
I thought poets were young.

SPOONER

I am young. (*He reaches for the bottle.*) Can I help you to a glass?

BRIGGS

No, thank you.

SPOONER *examines the bottle.*

SPOONER

An excellent choice.

BRIGGS

Not mine.

SPOONER

(*Pouring.*) Translating verse is an extremely difficult task. Only the Rumanians remain respectable exponents of the craft.

BRIGGS

Bit early in the morning for all this, isn't it?

SPOONER *drinks.*

Finish the bottle. Doctor's orders.

SPOONER

Can I enquire as to why I was locked in this room, by the way?

BRIGGS

Doctor's orders.

Pause

Tell me when you're ready for coffee.

Pause

It must be wonderful to be a poet and to have admirers. And translators. And to be young. I'm neither one nor the other.

SPOONER

Yes. You've reminded me. I must be off. I have a meeting at twelve. Thank you so much for breakfast.

BRIGGS

What meeting?

SPOONER

A board meeting. I'm on the board of a recently inaugurated poetry magazine. We have our first meeting at twelve. Can't be late.

BRIGGS

Where's the meeting?

SPOONER

At The Bull's Head in Chalk Farm. The landlord is kindly allowing us the use of a private room on the first floor. It is essential that the meeting be private, you see, as we shall be discussing policy.

BRIGGS

The Bull's Head in Chalk Farm?

SPOONER

Yes. The landlord is a friend of mine. It is on that account that he has favoured us with a private room. It is true of course that I informed him Lord Lancer would be attending the meeting. He at once appreciated that a certain degree of sequesteredness would be the order of the day.

BRIGGS

Lord Lancer?

SPOONER

Our patron.

BRIGGS

He's not one of the Bengal Lancers, is he?

SPOONER

No, no. He's of Norman descent.

BRIGGS

A man of culture?

SPOONER

Impeccable credentials.

BRIGGS

Some of these aristocrats hate the arts.

SPOONER

Lord Lancer is a man of honour. He loves the arts. He has declared this love in public. He never goes back on his word. But I must be off. Lord Lancer does not subscribe to the view that poets can treat time with nonchalance.

BRIGGS

Jack could do with a patron.

SPOONER

Jack?

BRIGGS

He's a poet.

SPOONER

A poet? Really? Well, if he'd like to send me some examples of
his work, double spaced on quarto, with copies in a separate
folder by separate post in case of loss or misappropriation,
stamped addressed envelope enclosed, I'll read them.

BRIGGS

That's very nice of you.

SPOONER

Not at all. You can tell him he can look forward to a scrupu-
lously honest and, if I may say so, highly sensitive judgement.

BRIGGS

I'll tell him. He's in real need of a patron. The boss could be
his patron, but he's not interested. Perhaps because he's a poet
himself. It's possible there's an element of jealousy in it, I
don't know. Not that the boss isn't a very kind man. He is.
He's a very civilised man. But he's still human.

Pause

SPOONER

The boss . . . is a poet himself?

BRIGGS

Don't be silly. He's more than that, isn't he? He's an essayist
and critic as well. He's a man of letters.

SPOONER

I thought his face was familiar.

The telephone buzzes. BRIGGS *goes to it, lifts it, listens.*

                    BRIGGS
Yes, sir.

BRIGGS *picks up the tray and takes it out.*

SPOONER *sits still.*

                    SPOONER
I have known this before. The voice unheard. A listener.
The command from an upper floor.

He pours champagne.

HIRST *enters, wearing a suit, followed by* BRIGGS.

                    HIRST
Charles. How nice of you to drop in.

He shakes SPOONER'*s hand.*

Have they been looking after you all right? Denson, let's have
some coffee.

BRIGGS *leaves the room.*

You're looking remarkably well. Haven't changed a bit. It's
the squash, I expect. Keeps you up to the mark. You were
quite a dab hand at Oxford, as I remember. Still at it? Wise
man. Sensible chap. My goodness, it's years. When did we last
meet? I have a suspicion we last dined together in '38, at the
club. Does that accord with your recollection? Croxley was
there, yes, Wyatt, it all comes back to me, Burston-Smith.

What a bunch. What a night, as I recall. All dead now, of
course. No, no! I'm a fool. I'm an idiot. Our last encounter – I
remember it well. Pavilion at Lord's in '39, against the West
Indies, Hutton and Compton batting superbly, Constantine
bowling, war looming. Surely I'm right? We shared a particularly fine bottle of port. You look as fit now as you did then.
Did you have a good war?

BRIGGS *comes in with coffee, places it on table.*

Oh thank you, Denson. Leave it there, will you? That will do.

BRIGGS *leaves the room.*

How's Emily? What a woman. (*Pouring.*) Black? Here you are.
What a woman. Have to tell you I fell in love with her once
upon a time. Have to confess it to you. Took her out to tea, in
Dorchester. Told her of my yearning. Decided to take the bull
by the horns. Proposed that she betray you. Admitted you
were a damn fine chap, but pointed out I would be taking
nothing that belonged to you, simply that portion of herself all
women keep in reserve, for a rainy day. Had an infernal job
persuading her. Said she adored you, her life would be mean-
ingless were she to be false. Plied her with buttered scones,
Wiltshire cream, crumpets and strawberries. Eventually she
succumbed. Don't suppose you ever knew about it, what?
Oh, we're too old now for it to matter, don't you agree?

He sits, with coffee.

I rented a little cottage for the summer. She used to motor to
me twice or thrice a week. I was an integral part of her shop-
ping expeditions. You were both living on the farm then. That's
right. Her father's farm. She would come to me at tea-time, or

at coffee-time, the innocent hours. That summer she was mine, while you imagined her to be solely yours.

He sips the coffee.

She loved the cottage. She loved the flowers. As did I. Narcissi, crocus, dog's tooth violets, fuchsia, jonquils, pinks, verbena.

Pause

Her delicate hands.

Pause

I'll never forget her way with jonquils.

Pause

Do you remember once, was it in '37, you took her to France? I was on the same boat. Kept to my cabin. While you were doing your exercises she came to me. Her ardour was, in my experience, unparalleled. Ah well.

Pause

You were always preoccupied with your physical . . condition . . weren't you? Don't blame you. Damn fine figure of a chap. Natural athlete. Medals, scrolls, your name inscribed in gold. Once a man has breasted the tape, alone, he is breasting the tape forever. His golden moment can never be tarnished. Do you run still? Why was it we saw so little of each other, after we came down from Oxford? I mean, you had another string to your bow, did you not? You were a literary man. As was I. Yes, yes, I know we shared the occasional picnic, with Tubby Wells and all that crowd, we shared the occasional whisky and soda at the club, but we were never close, were we? I wonder why. Of course I was successful awfully early.

Pause

You did say you had a good war, didn't you?

SPOONER

A rather good one, yes.

HIRST

How splendid. The RAF?

SPOONER

The Navy.

HIRST

How splendid. Destroyers?

SPOONER

Torpedo boats.

HIRST

First rate. Kill any Germans?

SPOONER

One or two.

HIRST

Well done.

SPOONER

And you?

HIRST

I was in Military Intelligence.

SPOONER

Ah.

Pause

HIRST

You pursued your literary career, after the war?

SPOONER

Oh yes.

HIRST

So did I.

SPOONER

I believe you've done rather well.

HIRST

Oh quite well, yes. Past my best now.

SPOONER

Do you ever see Stella?

Pause

HIRST

Stella?

SPOONER

You can't have forgotten.

HIRST

Stella who?

SPOONER

Stella Winstanley.

HIRST

Winstanley?

SPOONER

Bunty Winstanley's sister.

HIRST

Oh, Bunty. No, I never see her.

SPOONER

You were rather taken with her.

HIRST

Was I, old chap? How did you know?

SPOONER

I was terribly fond of Bunty. He was most dreadfully annoyed
with you. Wanted to punch you on the nose.

HIRST

What for?

SPOONER

For seducing his sister.

HIRST

What business was it of his?

SPOONER

He was her brother.

HIRST

That's my point.

Pause

What on earth are you driving at?

SPOONER

Bunty introduced Rupert to Stella. He was very fond of Rupert. He gave the bride away. He and Rupert were terribly old friends. He threatened to horsewhip you.

HIRST

Who did?

SPOONER

Bunty.

HIRST

He never had the guts to speak to me himself.

SPOONER

Stella begged him not to. She implored him to stay his hand. She implored him not to tell Rupert.

HIRST

I see. But who told Bunty?

SPOONER

I told Bunty. I was frightfully fond of Bunty. I was also frightfully fond of Stella.

Pause

HIRST

You appear to have been a close friend of the family.

SPOONER

Mainly of Arabella's. We used to ride together.

                     HIRST

Arabella Hinscott?

                     SPOONER

Yes.

                     HIRST

I knew her at Oxford.

                     SPOONER

So did I.

                     HIRST

I was very fond of Arabella.

                     SPOONER

Arabella was very fond of me. Bunty was never sure of precisely
how fond she was of me, nor of what form her fondness took.

                     HIRST

What in God's name do you mean?

                     SPOONER

Bunty trusted me. I was best man at their wedding. He also
trusted Arabella.

                     HIRST

I should warn you that I was always extremely fond of Arabella.
Her father was my tutor. I used to stay at their house.

                     SPOONER

I knew her father well. He took a great interest in me.

HIRST

Arabella was a girl of the most refined and organised sensibilities.

SPOONER

I agree.

Pause

HIRST

Are you trying to tell me that you had an affair with Arabella?

SPOONER

A form of an affair. She had no wish for full consummation. She was content with her particular predilection. Consuming the male member.

HIRST *stands.*

HIRST

I'm beginning to believe you're a scoundrel. How dare you speak of Arabella Hinscott in such a fashion? I'll have you blackballed from your club!

SPOONER

Oh my dear sir, may I remind you that you betrayed Stella Winstanley with Emily Spooner, my own wife, throughout a long and soiled summer, a fact known at the time throughout the Home Counties? May I further remind you that Muriel Blackwood and Doreen Busby have never recovered from your insane and corrosive sexual absolutism? May I further remind you that your friendship with and corruption of Geoffrey Ramsden at Oxford was the talk of Balliol and Christchurch Cathedral?

HIRST

This is scandalous! How dare you? I'll have you horse-whipped!

SPOONER

It is you, sir, who have behaved scandalously. To the fairest of sexes, of which my wife was the fairest representative. It is you who have behaved unnaturally and scandalously, to the woman who was joined to me in God.

HIRST

I, sir? Unnaturally? Scandalously?

SPOONER

Scandalously. She told me all.

HIRST

You listen to the drivellings of a farmer's wife?

SPOONER

Since I was the farmer, yes.

HIRST

You were no farmer, sir. A weekend wanker.

SPOONER

I wrote my Homage to Wessex in the summerhouse at West Upfield.

HIRST

I have never had the good fortune to read it.

SPOONER

It is written in terza rima, a form which, if you will forgive my saying so, you have never been able to master.

HIRST

This is outrageous! Who are you? What are you doing in my house?

He goes to the door and calls.

Denson! A whisky and soda!

He walks about the room.

You are clearly a lout. The Charles Wetherby I knew was a gentleman. I see a figure reduced. I am sorry for you. Where is the moral ardour that sustained you once? Gone down the hatch.

BRIGGS *enters, pours whisky and soda, gives it to* HIRST. HIRST *looks at it.*

Down the hatch. Right down the hatch. (*He drinks.*) I do not understand . . . I do not understand . . . and I see it all about me . . . continually . . . how the most sensitive and cultivated of men can so easily change, almost overnight, into the bully, the cutpurse, the brigand. In my day nobody changed. A man was. Only religion could alter him, and that at least was a glorious misery.

He drinks, and sits in his chair.

We are not banditti here. I am prepared to be patient. I shall be kind to you. I shall show you my library. I might even show you my study. I might even show you my pen, and my blottingpad. I might even show you my footstool.

He holds out his glass.

Another.

BRIGGS *takes glass, fills it, returns it.*

I might even show you my photograph album. You might even
see a face in it which might remind you of your own, of what
you once were. You might see faces of others, in shadow, or
cheeks of others, turning, or jaws, or backs of necks, or eyes,
dark under hats, which might remind you of others, whom
once you knew, whom you thought long dead, but from whom
you will still receive a sidelong glance, if you can face the good
ghost. Allow the love of the good ghost. They possess all that
emotion . . . trapped. Bow to it. It will assuredly never release
them, but who knows . . . what relief . . . it may give to
them . . . who knows how they may quicken . . . in their chains,
in their glass jars. You think it cruel . . . to quicken them, when
they are fixed, imprisoned? No. Deeply, deeply, they wish to
respond to your touch, to your look, and when you smile, their
joy . . . is unbounded. And so I say to you, tender the dead, as
you would yourself be tendered, now, in what you would
describe as your life.

He drinks.

BRIGGS
They're blank, mate, blank. The blank dead.

Silence

HIRST
Nonsense.

Pause

Pass the bottle.

                          BRIGGS

No.

                          HIRST

What?

                          BRIGGS

I said no.

                          HIRST

No pranks. No mischief. Give me the bottle.

Pause

                          BRIGGS

I've refused.

                          HIRST

Refusal can lead to dismissal.

                          BRIGGS

You can't dismiss me.

                          HIRST

Why not?

                          BRIGGS

Because I won't go.

                          HIRST

If I tell you to go, you will go. Give me the bottle.

Silence

HIRST *turns to* SPOONER.

HIRST

Bring me the bottle.

SPOONER *goes to cabinet.* BRIGGS *does not move.*
SPOONER *picks up whisky bottle, takes it to* HIRST.
HIRST *pours and places bottle at his side.*

BRIGGS

I'll have one myself.

BRIGGS *takes a glass to the bottle, pours and drinks.*

HIRST

What impertinence. Well, it doesn't matter. He was always a
scallywag. Is it raining? It so often rains, in August, in England.
Do you ever examine the gullies of the English countryside?
Under the twigs, under the dead leaves, you'll find tennis balls,
blackened. Girls threw them for their dogs, or children, for
each other, they rolled into the gully. They are lost there, given
up for dead, centuries old.

FOSTER *comes into the room.*

FOSTER

It's time for your morning walk.

Pause

I said it's time for your morning walk.

HIRST

My morning walk? No, no, I'm afraid I don't have the time
this morning.

FOSTER

It's time for your walk across the Heath.

HIRST

I can't possibly. I'm too busy. I have too many things to do.

FOSTER

What's that you're drinking?

SPOONER

The great malt which wounds.

HIRST

(*To* SPOONER.) My God, you haven't got a drink. Where's your glass?

SPOONER

Thank you. It would be unwise to mix my drinks.

HIRST

Mix?

SPOONER

I was drinking champagne.

HIRST

Of course you were, of course. Albert, another bottle.

BRIGGS

Certainly, sir.

BRIGGS *goes out.*

HIRST

I can't possibly. I have too many things to do. I have an essay to write. A critical essay. We'll have to check the files, find out what it is I'm supposed to be appraising. At the moment it's slipped my mind.

SPOONER

I could help you there.

HIRST

Oh?

SPOONER

On two counts. Firstly, I have the nose of a ferret. I can find anything in a file. Secondly, I have written any number of critical essays myself. Do you actually have a secretary?

FOSTER

I'm his secretary.

SPOONER

A secretarial post does less than justice to your talents. A young poet should travel. Travel and suffer. Join the navy, perhaps, and see the sea. Voyage and explore.

FOSTER

I've sailored. I've been there and back. I'm here where I'm needed.

BRIGGS *enters with champagne, stops at door, listens.*

SPOONER

(*To* HIRST.) You mentioned a photograph album. I could go through it with you. I could put names to the faces. A proper exhumation could take place. Yes, I am confident that I could be of enormous aid in that area.

FOSTER

Those faces are nameless, friend.

BRIGGS *comes into room, sets down champagne bucket.*

BRIGGS

And they'll always be nameless.

HIRST

There are places in my heart . . . where no living soul . . . has . . . or can ever . . . trespass.

BRIGGS *opens champagne, pours glass for* SPOONER.

BRIGGS

Here you are. Fresh as a daisy. (*To* HIRST.) A drop for you, sir?

HIRST

No, no. I'll stay . . . where I am.

BRIGGS

I'll join Mr. Friend, if I may, sir?

HIRST

Naturally.

BRIGGS

(*To* FOSTER.) Where's your glass?

FOSTER

No thanks.

HIRST

Oh come on, be sociable. Be sociable. Consort with the society to which you're attached. To which you're attached as if by bonds of steel. Mingle.

BRIGGS *pours a glass for* FOSTER.

FOSTER

It isn't even lunchtime.

BRIGGS

The best time to drink champagne is before lunch, you cunt.

FOSTER

Don't call me a cunt.

HIRST

We three, never forget, are the oldest of friends.

BRIGGS

That's why I called him a cunt.

FOSTER

(*To* BRIGGS.) Stop talking.

HIRST *lifts his glass.*

HIRST

To our good fortune.

Mutters of 'Cheers'. *They all drink.*
HIRST *looks at the window.*

HIRST

The light . . . out there . . . is gloomy . . . hardly daylight at all.
It is falling, rapidly. Distasteful. Let us close the curtains. Put
the lamps on.

BRIGGS *closes the curtains, lights lamps.*

HIRST

Ah. What relief.

Pause

How happy it is.

Pause

Today I shall come to a conclusion. There are certain matters
. . . which today I shall resolve.

SPOONER

I'll help you.

FOSTER

I was in Bali when they sent for me. I didn't have to leave, I
didn't have to come here. But I felt I was . . . called . . . I had
no alternative. I didn't have to leave that beautiful isle. But I
was intrigued. I was only a boy. But I was nondescript and
anonymous. A famous writer wanted me. He wanted me to be
his secretary, his chauffeur, his housekeeper, his amanuensis.
How did he know of me? Who told him?

SPOONER

He made an imaginative leap. Few can do it. Few do it. He did
it. And that's why God loves him.

BRIGGS

You came on my recommendation. I've always liked youth because you can use it. But it has to be open and honest. If it isn't open and honest you can't use it. I recommended you. You were open, the whole world before you.

FOSTER

I find the work fruitful. I'm in touch with a very special intelligence. This intelligence I find nourishing. I have been nourished by it. It's enlarged me. Therefore it's an intelligence worth serving. I find its demands natural. Not only that. They're legal. I'm not doing anything crooked. It's a relief. I could so easily have been bent. I have a sense of dignity in my work, a sense of honour. It never leaves me. Of service to a cause.

He refers to BRIGGS.

He is my associate. He was my proposer. I've learnt a great deal from him. He's been my guide. The most unselfish person I've ever met. He'll tell you. Let him speak.

BRIGGS

Who to?

FOSTER

What?

BRIGGS

Speak? Who to?

FOSTER *looks at* SPOONER.

FOSTER

To . . . him.

BRIGGS

To him? To a pisshole collector? To a shithouse operator?
To a jamrag vendor? What the fuck are you talking about?
Look at him. He's a mingejuice bottler, a fucking shitcake
baker. What are you talking to him for?

HIRST

Yes, yes, but he's a good man at heart. I knew him at Oxford.

Silence

SPOONER

(*To* HIRST.) Let me live with you and be your secretary.

HIRST

Is there a big fly in here? I hear buzzing.

SPOONER

No.

HIRST

You say no.

SPOONER

Yes.

Pause

I ask you . . . to consider me for the post. If I were wearing a
suit such as your own you would see me in a different light. I'm
extremely good with tradespeople, hawkers, canvassers, nuns.
I can be silent when desired or, when desired, convivial. I can
discuss any subject of your choice – the future of the country,
wild flowers, the Olympic Games. It is true I have fallen on

hard times, but my imagination and intelligence are unimpaired. My will to work has not been eroded. I remain capable of undertaking the gravest and most daunting responsibilities. Temperamentally I can be what you wish. My character is, at core, a humble one. I am an honest man and, moreover, I am not too old to learn. My cooking is not to be sneezed at. I lean towards French cuisine but food without frills is not beyond my competency. I have a keen eye for dust. My kitchen would be immaculate. I am tender towards objects. I would take good care of your silver. I play chess, billiards, and the piano. I could play Chopin for you. I could read the Bible to you. I am a good companion.

Pause

My career, I admit it freely, has been chequered. I was one of the golden of my generation. Something happened. I don't know what it was. Nevertheless I am I and have survived insult and deprivation. I am I. I offer myself not abjectly but with ancient pride. I come to you as a warrior. I shall be happy to serve you as my master. I bend my knee to your excellence. I am furnished with the qualities of piety, prudence, liberality and goodness. Decline them at your peril. It is my task as a gentleman to remain amiable in my behaviour, courageous in my undertakings, discreet and gallant in my executions, by which I mean your private life would remain your own. However, I shall be sensible to the least wrong offered you. My sword shall be ready to dissever all manifest embodiments of malign forces that conspire to your ruin. I shall regard it as incumbent upon me to preserve a clear countenance and a clean conscience. I will accept death's challenge on your behalf. I shall meet it, for your sake, boldly, whether it be in the field or in the bedchamber. I am your Chevalier. I had rather bury myself in a tomb of honour than permit your dignity to be sullied by domestic enemy or foreign foe. I am yours to command.

Silence

HIRST *is still, sitting.*
FOSTER *and* BRIGGS *are still, standing.*

SPOONER

Before you reply, I would like to say one thing more. I occasionally organise poetry readings, in the upstairs room of a particular public house. They are reasonably well attended, mainly by the young. I would be happy to offer you an evening of your own. You could read your own work, to an interested and informed audience, to an audience brimming over with potential for the greatest possible enthusiasm. I can guarantee a full house, and I will be happy to arrange a straightforward fee for you or, if you prefer, a substantial share of the profits. The young, I can assure you, would flock to hear you. My committee would deem it a singular honour to act as your host. You would be introduced by an authority on your work, perhaps myself. After the reading, which I am confident will be a remarkable success, we could repair to the bar below, where the landlord – who happens to be a friend of mine – would I know be overjoyed to entertain you, with the compliments of the house. Nearby is an Indian restaurant of excellent standing, at which you would be the guest of my committee. Your face is so seldom seen, your words, known to so many, have been so seldom heard, in the absolute authority of your own rendering, that this event would qualify for that rarest of categories: the unique. I beg you to consider seriously the social implications of such an adventure. You would be there in body. It would bring you to the young, the young to you. The elderly, also, those who have almost lost hope, would on this occasion leave their homes and present themselves. You would have no trouble with the press. I would take upon myself the charge of

keeping them from nuisance. Perhaps you might agree to half
a dozen photographs or so, but no more. Unless of course you
positively wished, on such an occasion, to speak. Unless you
preferred to hold, let us say, a small press conference, after the
reading, before supper, whereby you could speak through the
press to the world. But that is by the by, and would in no sense
be a condition. Let us content ourselves with the idea of an
intimate reading, in a pleasing and conducive environment, let
us consider an evening to be remembered, by all who take
part in her.

Silence

HIRST

Let us change the subject.

Pause

For the last time.

Pause

What have I said?

FOSTER

You said you're changing the subject for the last time.

HIRST

But what does that mean?

FOSTER

It means you'll never change the subject again.

HIRST

Never?

FOSTER

Never.

HIRST

Never?

FOSTER

You said for the last time.

HIRST

But what does that *mean*? What does it *mean*?

FOSTER

It means forever. It means that the subject is changed once and for all and for the last time forever. If the subject is winter, for instance, it'll be winter forever.

HIRST

Is the subject winter?

FOSTER

The subject is now winter. So it'll therefore be winter forever.

BRIGGS

And for the last time.

FOSTER

Which will last forever. If the subject is winter, for example, spring will never come.

HIRST

But let me ask you – I must ask you –

FOSTER

Summer will never come.

BRIGGS

The trees –

FOSTER

Will never bud.

HIRST

I must ask you –

BRIGGS

Snow –

FOSTER

Will fall forever. Because you've changed the subject. For the last time.

HIRST

But have we? That's my question. Have I? Have we changed the subject?

FOSTER

Of course. The previous subject is closed.

HIRST

What was the previous subject?

FOSTER

It's forgotten. You've changed it.

HIRST

What is the present subject?

FOSTER

That there is no possibility of changing the subject since the subject has now been changed.

BRIGGS

For the last time.

FOSTER

So that nothing else will happen forever. You'll simply be sitting here forever.

BRIGGS

But not alone.

FOSTER

No. We'll be with you. Briggs and me.

Pause

HIRST

It's night.

FOSTER

And will always be night.

BRIGGS

Because the subject –

FOSTER

Can never be changed.

Silence

HIRST

But I hear sounds of birds. Don't you hear them? Sounds I never heard before. I hear them as they must have sounded then, when I was young, although I never heard them then, although they sounded about us then.

Pause

Yes. It is true. I am walking towards a lake. Someone is following me, through the trees. I lose him, easily. I see a body in the water, floating. I am excited. I look closer and see I was mistaken. There is nothing in the water. I say to myself, I saw a body, drowning. But I am mistaken. There is nothing there.

Silence

SPOONER
No. You are in no man's land. Which never moves, which never changes, which never grows older, but which remains forever, icy and silent.

Silence

HIRST
I'll drink to that.

He drinks.

SLOW FADE

Selected List of Grove Press Drama and Theater Paperbacks

E471   BECKETT, SAMUEL / Cascando and Other Short Dramatic Pieces (Words and Music, Film, Play, Come and Go, Eh Joe, Endgame) / $1.95

E96   BECKETT, SAMUEL / Endgame / $1.95

E318   BECKETT, SAMUEL / Happy Days / $2.45

E226   BECKETT, SAMUEL / Krapp's Last Tape, plus All That Fall, Embers, Act Without Words I and II / $2.45

E33   BECKETT, SAMUEL / Waiting For Godot / $1.95 [See also Seven Plays of the Modern Theater, Harold Clurman, ed. GT422 / $4.95]

B117   BRECHT, BERTOLT / The Good Woman of Setzuan / $1.95

B108   BRECHT, BERTOLT / Mother Courage and Her Children / $1.50

B333   BRECHT, BERTOLT / The Threepenny Opera / $1.45

E130   GENET, JEAN / The Balcony / $2.95 [See also Seven Plays of the Modern Theater, Harold Clurman, ed. GT422 / $4.95]

E208   GENET, JEAN / The Blacks: A Clown Show / $2.95

E577   GENET, JEAN / The Maids and Deathwatch: Two Plays / $2.95

E374   GENET, JEAN / The Screens / $1.95

E101   IONESCO, EUGENE / Four Plays (The Bald Soprano, The Lesson, The Chairs,* Jack, or The Submission) / $1.95 *[See also Eleven Short Plays of the Modern Theater, Samuel Moon, ed. B107 / $2.45]

E259   IONESCO, EUGENE / Rhinoceros* and Other Plays (The Leader, The Future is in Eggs, or It Takes All Sorts to Make a World) / $1.95 *[See also Seven Plays of the Modern Theater, Harold Clurman, ed. GT422 / $4.95]

E119   IONESCO, EUGENE / Three Plays (Amédée, The New Tenant, Victims of Duty) / $2.95

B354   PINTER, HAROLD / Old Times / $1.95

E299   PINTER, HAROLD / The Caretaker* and The Dumb Waiter: Two Plays / $1.95 *[See also Modern British Drama, Henry Popkin, ed. GT422 / $5.95]

E411   PINTER, HAROLD / The Homecoming / $1.95

E626   STOPPARD, TOM / Jumpers / $1.95

B319   STOPPARD, TOM / Rosencrantz and Guildenstern Are Dead / $1.95

GROVE PRESS, INC., 53 East 11th Street, New York, N.Y. 10003